THIS BOOK BELONGS TO:

_____

_____

_____

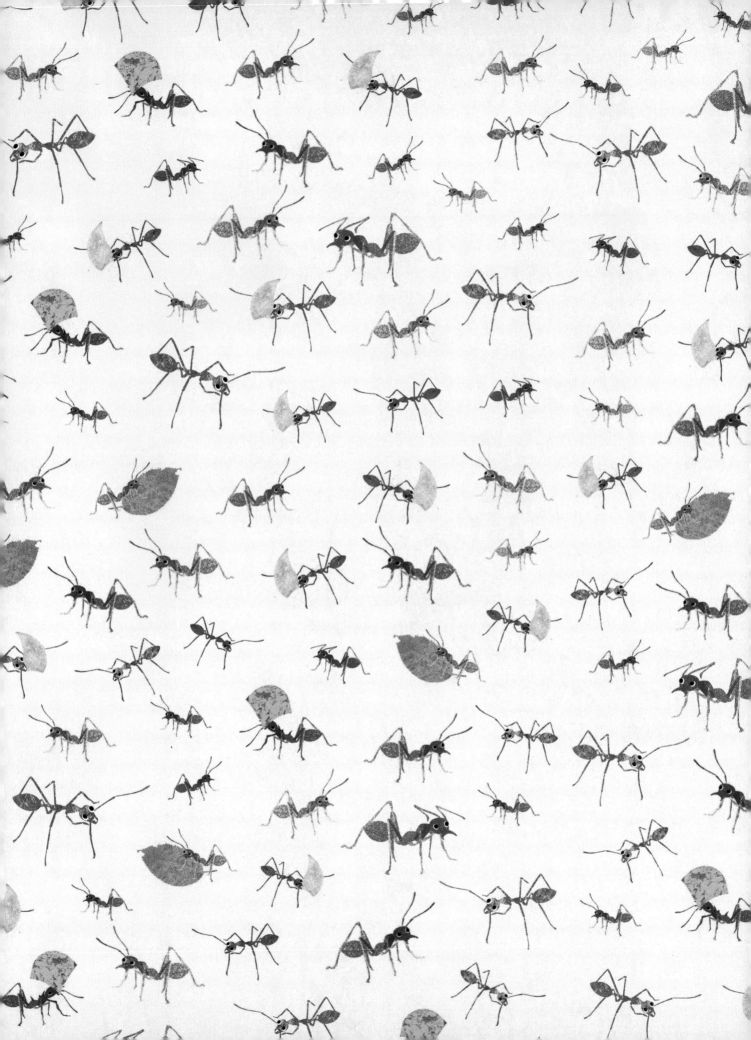

First US paperback edition 2024
First published by Big Picture Press,
an imprint of Bonnier Books UK, 2019

Library of Congress Catalog Card Number 2020902060
ISBN 978-1-5362-1042-2 (hardcover)
ISBN 978-1-5362-3502-9 (paperback)

24 25 26 27 28 29 TLF 10 9 8 7 6 5 4 3 2 1

Printed in Dongguan, Guangdong, China

This book was typeset in Core Circus
Rough and Neutraface Text.
The illustrations were created digitally.

BIG PICTURE PRESS
an imprint of
Candlewick Press
99 Dover Street
Somerville, Massachusetts 02144

www.candlewick.com

BUGS

EVERYWHERE

ILLUSTRATED BY BRITTA TECKENTRUP
WRITTEN BY LILY MURRAY

B P P

THERE ARE BUGS EVERYWHERE

The world is alive with bugs. There are millions of different species. In fact, there are so many that no one knows the exact number. You can find bugs almost anywhere—scurrying underground, fluttering through the air, or gliding through water. Hundreds live in your house and some even live on your skin!

Spider

Horsefly

Twenty-two-spotted ladybug

Seven-spotted ladybug

Dragonfly

Chan's megastick

Cicada

Mosquito

Stinkbug

Orchid mantis

Centipede

Horned dung beetle

Striped shield bug

Scorpion

Peacock butterfly

Madagascan sunset moth

Wasp

Winged termite

Hewitson's saber-wing butterfly

Swallowtail butterfly

Honeybee

Mayfly

Japanese boxer mantis

Cockroach

Grasshopper

Stinging rose caterpillar

Giant leaf katydid

Leaf-cutter ant

Titan longhorn beetle

Some of these bugs are record breakers! Which bug do you think is the strongest? Now see if you can guess which is the longest, the noisiest, and the fastest flyer.

IT'S A BUG!
(SO WHAT *IS* THAT?)

The creatures that we call bugs belong to a group known as arthropods. All arthropods have six or more legs, and their bodies are divided into parts (or segments). They also have a hard outer covering called an exoskeleton.

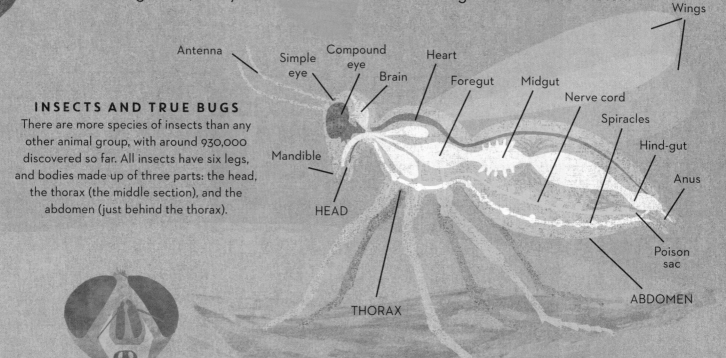

Antenna · Simple eye · Compound eye · Brain · Heart · Foregut · Midgut · Nerve cord · Spiracles · Hind-gut · Anus · Wings · Mandible · HEAD · THORAX · Poison sac · ABDOMEN

INSECTS AND TRUE BUGS

There are more species of insects than any other animal group, with around 930,000 discovered so far. All insects have six legs, and bodies made up of three parts: the head, the thorax (the middle section), and the abdomen (just behind the thorax).

HOW BUGS SEE

Most bugs have large eyes, known as **compound eyes,** made up of lots of different light sensors. These help bugs to detect movement, but they make it harder to spot smaller details. Many arthropods can also have **ocelli,** or simple eyes, which detect changes in light.

TRUE BUGS

True bugs are a group of insects that includes shield bugs, assassin bugs, and bedbugs. All true bugs have a beak, which they use to pierce and suck on their food.

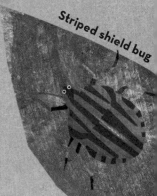

Striped shield bug

RECORD BREAKERS

Did you guess which bugs on the last page were record breakers?

The **horned dung beetle** is the world's strongest bug. It can pull up to 1,141 times its own weight—that's the same as a person lifting six double-decker buses!

The **horsefly** is the fastest flying bug, reaching speeds of up to 90 miles/145 kilometers per hour.

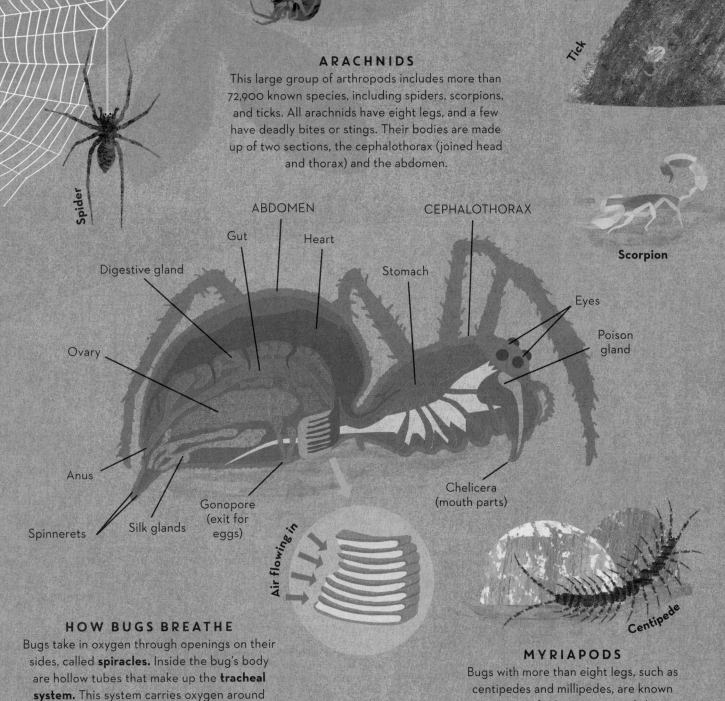

ARACHNIDS

This large group of arthropods includes more than 72,900 known species, including spiders, scorpions, and ticks. All arachnids have eight legs, and a few have deadly bites or stings. Their bodies are made up of two sections, the cephalothorax (joined head and thorax) and the abdomen.

Tick

Spider

ABDOMEN

CEPHALOTHORAX

Gut

Heart

Stomach

Digestive gland

Scorpion

Ovary

Eyes

Poison gland

Anus

Spinnerets

Silk glands

Gonopore (exit for eggs)

Chelicera (mouth parts)

Air flowing in

Centipede

HOW BUGS BREATHE

Bugs take in oxygen through openings on their sides, called **spiracles.** Inside the bug's body are hollow tubes that make up the **tracheal system.** This system carries oxygen around the bug's body and carbon dioxide back out through the spiracles.

MYRIAPODS

Bugs with more than eight legs, such as centipedes and millipedes, are known as **myriapods.** Some myriapods have more than 700 legs!

The **cicada** is the loudest insect in the world. A swarm can make sounds of up to 106 decibels — about as loud as a rock concert!

Chan's megastick is the longest bug in the world. It lives in the rain forests of Borneo and can grow up to 22 inches/56 centimeters long!

BUGS HAVE BEEN AROUND FOR AGES

Bugs have been around for a really long time. There have been arthropods in the oceans for over 500 million years. Then, around 480 million years ago, insects' ancestors were among the first animals on land. There was even a time, known as the Carboniferous period (360 to 285 million years ago), when giant bugs roamed the Earth.

Isotelus

500 million years ago

Trilobites are among the earliest known arthropods. Most were tiny, but some, such as *Isotelus,* grew up to 28 inches/ 70 centimeters long.

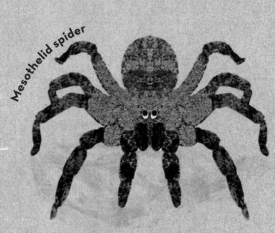

Mesothelid spider

Mesothelid spiders are living fossils in today's world. Their ancestors first appeared around 400 million years ago.

Meganeura

Meganeura lived around 300 million years ago and grew to the size of a seagull.

Oxygen levels 300 million years ago were very high, and bugs grew to enormous sizes. At 7½ feet/2.3 meters long, **Arthropleura** was one of the biggest bugs that ever existed.

Silverfish

Silverfish are very ancient insects. The ones that lived around 200 million years ago are very similar to the ones alive today.

Arthropleura

The first insects most likely evolved from a group of venomous crustaceans called **remipedes.** Remipedes are still alive today. They are completely blind and live in underwater caves.

Remipede

Hibbertopterus

Scorpions first crawled out of the water around 430 million years ago. Early scorpions, such as **Hibbertopterus,** spent most of their lives at sea but also had feet to scuttle around on land.

Mayfly

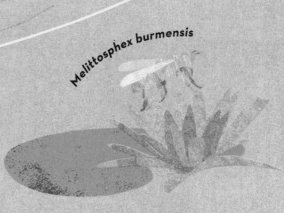

Melittosphex burmensis

Around 400 million years ago, insects were the first creatures to fly. Plants were growing taller, and flying enabled insects to reach their food source. The first flying insects may have been the ancestors of today's **mayflies.**

The Cretaceous period (144 to 64 million years ago) brought flowering plants and bugs that fed on them—including butterflies, ants, and the first known species of bee, **Melittosphex burmensis.**

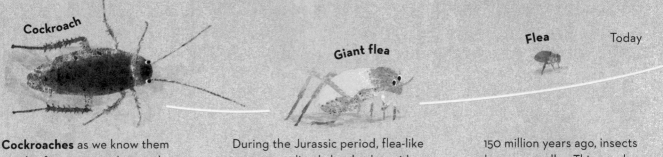

Cockroach

Giant flea

Flea   Today

Cockroaches as we know them today first appeared around 180 million years ago.

During the Jurassic period, flea-like creatures lived closely alongside dinosaurs. They were ten times the size of fleas today.

150 million years ago, insects became smaller. This may be because birds took to the skies and smaller insects could make a quicker escape.

WHERE DO BUGS LIVE?

Dragonfly

Dragonfly

There are very few places bugs don't live! You can find them in rain forests, deserts, woodlands, wetlands, caves, grasslands, in the freezing Antarctic, and in your own backyard. Bugs, in fact, live in more habitats than any other animal group on Earth.

WATER BUGS

Many bugs live in ponds, lakes, streams, or rivers, and you can even find insects in the tiniest pools of water — or above them! **Dragonflies** zoom over water, catching insects in the air.

Water spider

Great diving beetle

Water spiders spend most of their lives underwater but still need air to breathe. They come to the surface to collect large air bubbles, which they live in during the day. They leave their bubbles to hunt at night.

Great diving beetles live underwater where they hunt for bugs, tadpoles, and even fish. To breathe, they trap air bubbles under their wings.

Great pond snail

The great pond snail glides over surfaces on its slimy, muscular foot. Its tongue is studded with tiny teeth, which it uses to feed on algae and plant and animal matter.

DESERT BUGS

Most animals struggle to survive in deserts because of the lack of water. Many species of bugs, however, have developed amazing adaptations to live in these hostile environments.

The **darkling beetle** survives in the harshest of deserts. On cool mornings it runs to the top of sand dunes, where it stands on its head to collect water from fog, which rolls down to its mouth!

ALPINE BUGS

In the mountains, temperatures can be extremely cold. Many bugs that live there are dark-colored, which helps them absorb the sun's heat.

The dark-gray grasshopper *Sigaus villosus* lives in mountains in New Zealand. It uses its long back legs like ski poles when it walks across snow.

POLAR BUGS

Since there are no land mammals in Antarctica, bugs are the largest animals on land—making **springtails** and **mites** Antarctica's most fearsome land predators!

The **rhagidia mite** is about 1 millimeter wide and feeds on microscopic creatures. Its body produces a substance called glycerol, which keeps it from freezing.

UNDERGROUND BUGS

Bugs that live in soil feed on plants and animals (alive or dead) and dung. Many live underground their whole lives, some just hibernate there, and others live there only when they're young.

Mole crickets spend most of their lives underground. Like moles, they have huge, shovel-like front legs for digging, either to find food or to make a chamber for their eggs.

RAIN FORESTS

The Amazon in South America, like rain forests everywhere, contains mind-blowing numbers of arthropods. A single square mile can be home to more than 50,000 different species! Each species performs a vital role in the survival of the forest. Without these bugs, rain forests as we know them would not exist.

EMERGENT LAYER
Huge umbrella-shaped trees, more than 250 feet/75 meters high, form the **emergent layer.** Butterflies flit from flower to flower spreading pollen.

CANOPY LAYER
The **canopy layer** sits hundreds of feet above the ground. The many flowers here attract insects such as bees, beetles, and wasps.

UNDERSTORY
Below the canopy lies the **understory.** Thick and dense with plant life, this layer is home to countless insects, including bees and stick insects.

Hewitson's saber-wing butterfly

Hewitson's saber-wing butterflies move so fast that the human eye can't follow them.

Leafcutter ants harvest leaves from the canopy and carry them down to their nests.

Blue morpho butterflies drink juice from rotting fruit, dead animals, and fungi, and spread spores (from which new fungi will form) around the forest.

Leafcutter ants

Blue morpho butterfly

Leaf beetles

Orchid bees

Orchid bees travel through the understory collecting scent from orchids.

CAN YOU FIND?

Bugs are an important food source for many rain forest animals. How many animals that prey on insects can you find on this page?

The **goliath bird-eating tarantula** has a leg span of up to 11 inches/28 centimeters and can easily hunt small birds and frogs. It uses its huge fangs to inject prey with venom!

Goliath bird-eating tarantula

Most stick insects are masters of disguise. However, the **Peruvian fire stick** is brightly colored.

Peruvian fire stick

Glowworm

When **click beetles** are in their larval stage, they are one of the insects commonly called *glowworms*. They make their own light via a process called bioluminescence, which attracts termites that the glowworms then eat.

Bullet ant

Bullet ants can be aggressive if their colony is under threat. They have one of the most painful stings of any insect.

The **Titan longhorn beetle** is one of the world's largest beetles, at 6½ inches/16.5 centimeters long. Its powerful jaws could snap a pencil in two.

Titan longhorn beetle

Termites

FOREST FLOOR

Very little light reaches the forest floor. Spiders and beetles crawl along the ground, which is covered in fallen leaves, rotting twigs, and shallow roots.

Termites live in huge colonies on the forest floor. They munch up wood and mix it with their excrement, creating fungus gardens for them to feed from.

Termite mound

FEEDING

Bugs feast on an amazing array of different foods, including plants, other bugs, dead flesh, rotting materials, and even dung! It may sound disgusting, but bugs' feeding habits play a very important role in the natural world.

POOP EATERS

Dung beetles may eat excrement, but they are fussy about the poop they eat. Some will only eat the dung of one species of animal. They feed by sucking up nutritious moisture from the dung.

FOOD GROWERS

Leafcutter ants slice leaves with saw-toothed jaws that vibra 1,000 times a second. The decaying leaves grow into a fungu which feeds the entire colony.

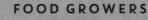

PLANT MUNCHERS

Caterpillars have tough, sharp mandibles, or jaws, which they use to munch through leaves.

CARNIVOROUS BUGS

Dragonflies hunt for midges and mosquitoes. Their compoun eyes contain as many as 28,000 lenses, which help them to look in many directions at once.

NECTAR DRINKERS

The **hummingbird hawk moth** has a long tongue for slurping nectar from deep, tube-shaped flowers. Its wings beat 80 times a second, so it can hover while feeding.

SPONGY MOUTHS

Houseflies and **bluebottles** can't bite or chew. Instead, they cover their food in saliva, which turns it into a liquid. They then suck it up using spongy pads on their mouths.

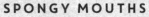

SWARMS

Sometimes plant-eating bugs join together in huge numbers, destroying the food crops that people rely on. The most famous swarming bug is the desert locust.

Locust swarms have impacted humans for thousands of years. There are stories of these swarms in the Bible and in writings by ancient Egyptians.

When there is an explosion in grasshopper numbers, they come together, forming vast swarms of millions of individuals.

When they live alone, locusts are known as **grasshoppers.** Their excrement fertilizes soil, and they are a vital source of food for many creatures, including birds, spiders, and small mammals.

Each locust can eat its own body weight in plants and travel vast distances in a day. In 1954, a swarm flew all the way from northwest Africa to Great Britain!

COMMUNAL LIVING

Many species of insects, including termites, bees, wasps, and ants, live together in large groups known as colonies. Insects in colonies lead very organized lives, working together to produce food, care for their young, and protect one another against predators.

Honeybee colonies sometimes contain tens of thousands of individuals. They each have different jobs to do.

Female bees create wax from their **wax glands,** which they use to build the nest. The nest is full of little pockets called **cells.**

The young, or larvae, are raised in cells known as **brood chambers.** When the larvae are fully grown, they spin **cocoons** for themselves.

Females become **worker bees.** The youngest, known as **nurse bees,** feed bee bread (a mixture of pollen and honey) to the larvae.

The **queen bee** gives off chemicals, called **pheromones,** which control the other bees, and ensure that she is the only bee in the colony to lay eggs.

CAN YOU FIND?
Wasps often blend in with swarms of bees so they can sneak into the hive and raid it. Can you spot two wasps hiding in this hive?

Older worker bees, called **foragers,** visit flowers to collect nectar, which they suck up through their long tongues.

Male bees become **drones,** whose sole purpose is to mate with a queen. They die shortly after mating.

When a bee visits a flower, pollen sticks to hairs on its body. It brushes the pollen into pouches on its back legs called **pollen baskets.**

Pollen is mainly used to feed to the larvae, while nectar is turned into **honey,** the bees' winter food.

STAYING ALIVE

Bugs live near the bottom of the food chain, so there are lots of animals that want to eat them! This means they have had to develop tricky ways of avoiding predators, such as playing dead or mimicking their surroundings. Some bugs are almost impossible to spot!

CAN YOU FIND?

These bugs are great at camouflage.
Where are they hiding? Look for:
Orchid mantis — looks like a flower
Chan's megastick — looks like a stick
Giant leaf katydid — looks like a leaf

MASTERS OF SURVIVAL

SCARY EYES

When startled, the **elephant hawk moth caterpillar** puffs out its body, making its eyespots look like snake eyes. This fools predators into thinking they are looking at a much scarier creature.

The bright, contrasting eyespots of a **peacock butterfly** can startle birds and give the butterfly more time to escape.

TOXIC WARNING

A **ladybug's** striking red-and-black coloring warns predators that it can release a stinky and foul-tasting chemical if attacked.

LET'S PRETEND

To avoid being eaten, **click beetles** lie on their back and pretend to be dead. They can then quickly escape by flexing a hinge in their body that hurls them up into the air, producing a loud clicking sound.

Ladybug

Ladybug mimic spider

The **ladybug mimic spider** has evolved a similar color pattern to that of ladybugs. This keeps predators away — even though these mimics don't actually taste bad!

POISONOUS BRISTLES

Some caterpillars, such as the **stinging rose caterpillar,** are covered in stinging hairs. These act as a defense against birds and predatory insects.

STRANGE HATS

When a **gum leaf skeletonizer** caterpillar molts, or sheds its skin, it keeps the casing that once covered its head. With each molt, the stack of empty head cases grows until it forms a tower, which it uses to deter predators like stinkbugs.

Stinkbug

TRICKY HUNTERS

Spiders are excellent hunters. Some hide and then pounce on their prey, while many make intricate silk webs to catch their food.

Like all spiders, **golden orb weavers** produce silk in their abdomen. To make a web, they squeeze the silk out of little holes, called **spinnerets,** on the underside of their body.

The female golden orb weaver is larger than the male and can build huge wheel-shaped webs, sometimes more than 3 feet/1 meter across!

Golden orb weavers prey mainly on insects, but their webs can be strong enough to catch bats and small birds.

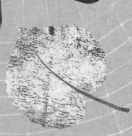

Females often spin rotting leaves or other plant debris into their webs to attract prey.

CAN YOU FIND?
It looks like some prey has fallen victim to this spider's huge web! Can you find the trapped creatures, which the spider can eat for its dinner?

When something lands on the web, the spider plucks the web's silk strings. The vibrations help the spider determine what prey it has caught.

The spider also adds in web decorations, known as **stabilimenta,** often in a zigzag pattern. They reflect ultraviolet light and act as insect lures.

Golden orb weavers get their name from the bright color of their webs.

The golden orb weaver paralyzes its prey by injecting it with venom from its fangs. It then wraps its meal in a silk cocoon to store it for later.

AMAZING WEBS

Funnel web spiders use their webs as both traps and hideouts. Silk trip lines at the front of the funnel alert the spider to prey.

Cobweb spiders make irregular, sticky webs. When an insect gets stuck in the web, the spider injects it with venom, wraps it in silk, and saves it for later.

Some spiders build **woolly webs** out of silk that isn't sticky. To trap their prey, the spiders give the silk an electric charge by brushing it repeatedly with their back legs.

BUG PARENTS

Bugs will go to all sorts of lengths to attract a mate. Some dance, others bring gifts, and a few even risk their lives. Once their bug babies are born, many parents leave their offspring to fend for themselves. However, some stick around for years, attentively caring for their young.

EAT MY WINGS

A male **hump-winged grig** rubs his forewings together to attract a mate. He then allows the female to munch on his wings and lap up the blood-like fluid called hemolymph.

GRUESOME GIFTS

Some species of male **balloon flies** wrap a dead insect inside an oval balloon of silk and then dance around with it. A female flies into the swarm and chooses her partner, who then offers her his gift.

SMELLY SURPRISE

Female **emperor moths** produce a scent called a pheromone to attract mates. Males can pick up the scent with their feathery antennae from up to 5 miles/8 kilometers away.

A RISKY DANCE

Male **peacock jumping spiders** dance to impress females. They move their legs, vibrate their bodies, and unfurl their elaborate fan, revealing its striking shape and colors. This is a very dangerous dance, because if the female doesn't want to mate with him, she will eat him instead!

Male

Peacock jumping spiders

Female

A MEAL FOR TWO

Wood-burrowing cockroaches live in nests that they keep clean and defend. They care for their young for at least three years, feeding them by chewing food and spitting it out, a process called regurgitation.

A WATCHFUL EYE

Stinkbug mothers guard their eggs, covering them with their bodies to protect them from parasitic wasps that want to lay their own eggs in them.

CICADA LIFE CYCLE

Adult male **cicadas** spend their days calling out for a mate. They make loud chirping and clicking noises to attract females as far away as 1 mile/ 1.6 kilometers away!

When the female cicada is ready to lay her eggs, she cuts a groove in a branch of a tree, deposits her eggs there, and then leaves.

When the conditions are right, the nymphs climb up trees. They shed their exoskeleton, emerging as fully grown adults with wings, ready to search for a mate.

Young cicadas are called **nymphs.** When they first hatch, they are about the size of a grain of rice. They fall to the ground and burrow into the soil.

Cicada nymphs live underground for up to 17 years, sucking sap from tree roots.

Cicada nymphs

Nymphs are young bugs that look like small adults without wings. The young of some types of bugs, such as bees, look very different from the adults and are known as **larvae.**

MADAGASCAN SUNSET MOTHS

Madagascan sunset moths live only in Madagascar, an island off the east coast of southern Africa. With their vibrant, colorful wings, they are considered one of the most beautiful moths in the world. Despite their delicate wings, each year they migrate huge distances across Madagascar in the thousands in search of plants on which to lay their eggs.

Eggs

Madagascan sunset moth

After **Madagascan sunset moths** complete their long migration, the females lay their eggs. Each moth lays around 80 domed eggs on the undersides of **Omphalea** leaves, the only plant their caterpillars will eat.

The eggs hatch into yellow-and-white caterpillars with black spots and bristle-like hairs.

Omphalea leaves contain **toxins** that don't harm the caterpillars, but protect them from predators such as ants and birds. The caterpillars can quickly devour entire plants.

Caterpillars

CAN YOU FIND?

Madagascan sunset moths like to drink nectar from all kinds of plants — their favorites have white or yellow flowers. How many moths can you spot slurping up nectar with their long, straw-like tongues?

The *Omphalea* plants the moths left behind on the other side of the island slowly become less toxic. This means the moths can one day return.

When the moths finally find a new patch of the *Omphalea* plant, they settle to breed and the cycle begins once again.

They spin a cocoon made from silk around themselves.

Cocoon

At two months old, the caterpillars are ready to transform.

After 17 to 23 days, they emerge as moths.

The moths let their wings dry for up to two hours. Then they can fly.

Before their transformation, the caterpillars spend weeks eating *Omphalea* leaves. In response the plants begin to develop a stronger toxin, which can harm the caterpillars.

The moths must now find new plants. They migrate all the way across Madagascar, from the rain forests in the east to the dry forests in the west, flying over mountains and semideserts.

Madagascan sunset moths fly during the day. By night, they roost together for warmth and protection.

The moths have few predators, as their bright colors act as a warning that they are toxic to eat. As the moths fly, their wings appear to change color, but this is just an illusion.

BUGS AND PEOPLE

Bugs have been vital to humans for millions of years. They fertilize plants, break down waste, and are an important food source for animals and humans. Throughout history, humans have feared bugs but have also been inspired by them. We are only just beginning to realize that bugs are essential to the future of the planet.

BUG CHARMS
In ancient Egypt, **scarab beetles** were symbols of Khepri the sun god and new life. The scarab was a popular design for jewelry, charms, and stamps, and many scarab amulets have been found buried with mummies.

ANCIENT FOOD
Our hunter-gatherer ancestors relied on bugs for protein. For the ancient Romans, wine-fed **beetle larvae** were a delicacy. Today, many people still eat bugs, and as our population grows, bugs could become a key, and environmentally friendly, food source.

TUNEFUL PETS
Since as far back as 1000 BCE, the Chinese have kept **crickets** as pets, often in elaborate bamboo or metal cages. These insects were cherished for their singing, which they actually produce by rubbing their wings together.

BUG INVENTIONS

Today, research into bugs is at the cutting edge of science. It has led to some fascinating solutions to human problems, which will help shape our future.

The **bombardier beetle** blasts toxic steam from its abdomen. Scientists studying it have developed a new type of needle-free injection.

Termite mounds do not overheat in the sun due to a system of air pockets that circulate cool air. This trick has inspired the design of a shopping mall in Zimbabwe, which uses a similar system of air pockets to keep cool.

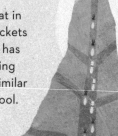

A WORLD
WITHOUT BUGS

Bugs are an invisible power that keeps the world working. But they are under threat, and their numbers are dwindling. So how do we protect them? Here are a few things you can do at home.

Plant nectar-rich flowers, such as buddleia and autumn ivy, for **butterflies** and **bees** to feed on.

Why not make a bug hotel filled with dry leaves, dead wood, and hollow tubes? It will make an ideal home for **beetles, centipedes, spiders,** and more.

Dig a pond! It will attract insects such as **dragonflies, pond skaters,** and **water beetles.**

Scientists predict that millions more species of bugs are yet to be discovered. So get out your magnifying glass and see if you can find the next new species of insect, arachnid, or myriapod!

Spider silk is stronger than steel and is tough, light, and flexible. An artificial version has been created and is used in medical equipment, machine parts, and protective clothing for soldiers.

Dragonflies can spot moving objects in the dark. Scientists are studying these insects to see if they can build tiny flying robots with the same abilities.

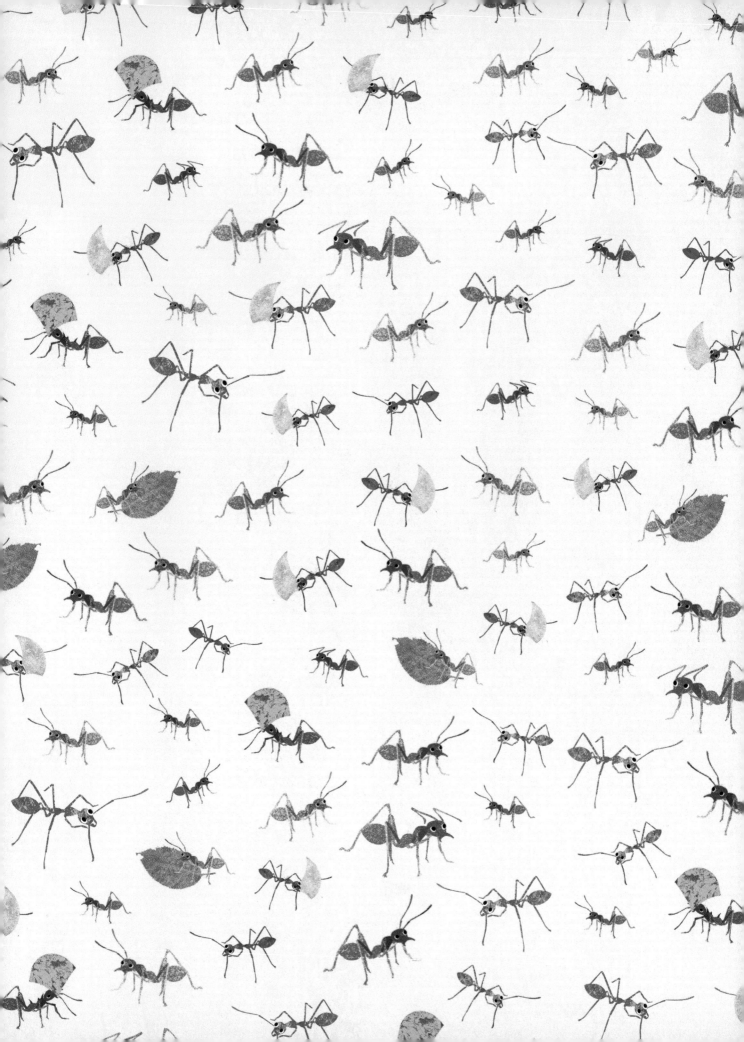

CAN YOU FIND?

The golden tortoise beetle from North America only grows to around 7 millimeters long, but it has a powerful survival strategy. When under attack, it can change color, from gold to orange to spotted black to brown. There is a golden tortoise beetle hiding somewhere in this book. Can you find it?

There are Animals Everywhere!
Read them all.

ILLUSTRATED BY BRITTA TECKENTRUP

Fish Everywhere
Available in paperback!

Put on your diving goggles and plunge underwater. See rivers where salmon leap and explore reefs where parrotfish munch on coral. Best-selling illustrator Britta Teckentrup brings the fascinating world of fish to life in vibrant color.

Hardcover ISBN 978-1-5362-0625-8
Paperback ISBN 978-1-5362-3264-6

Bugs Everywhere
Available in paperback!

Dig out your magnifying glass and explore the world of bugs. Venture into rain forests where tarantulas hunt, and peek inside hives where busy bees work. Best-selling illustrator Britta Teckentrup brings these amazing creatures to life in vibrant color.

Hardcover ISBN 978-1-5362-1042-2
Paperback ISBN 978-1-5362-3502-9

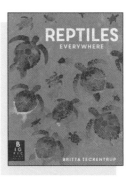

Reptiles Everywhere
Available in paperback!

Pull on your boots and get ready to track down some reptiles. Follow geckos through the Madagascan jungle and take a stroll down to the beach to watch baby turtles hatch. Best-selling illustrator Britta Teckentrup brings the mesmerizing world of reptiles to life in vibrant color.

Hardcover ISBN 978-1-5362-1707-0
Paperback ISBN 978-1-5362-3265-3

Birds Everywhere

Grab your binoculars and get ready to go bird-watching. Spy eagles soaring through the sky and follow emperor penguins as they brave freezing temperatures on their icy journey to the ocean. Best-selling illustrator Britta Teckentrup brings these aviators to life in vibrant color.

Hardcover ISBN 978-1-5362-2973-8

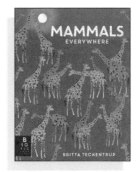

Mammals Everywhere

Put on your backpack and get ready to track down some mammals. Follow a pride of lions across the savanna and spot a polar bear hidden in the Arctic landscape. Best-selling illustrator Britta Teckentrup brings the wide variety of mammals to life in vibrant color.

Hardcover ISBN 978-1-5362-3262-2